FIVE TRUTHS
for thinking about
DIFFICULT
PEOPLE

Kris Plachy, MA, Master Coach

Illustrated by Steven Hall | stevenhalldesign.com

LEADERSHIP COACH
—— INC ——

Five Truths for Thinking About Difficult People

In a perfect world, it would be easy to work along side one another. But the truth is we all have significant differences in how we think about the world. Those differences lead us to behaving differently than one another. What may be acceptable to you or me may not be acceptable for someone else.

Because trying to change other people is an exercise in futility, we have created a quick guide to help **you** help **yourself** as you navigate challenging relationships.

When we become masters of our own minds and our own behaviors, we take huge strides towards changing how we relate.

How to Use This Guide

What you'll find inside are **five** invitations.

These invitations are designed to challenge your thinking and **invite** you to try on something you may not have thought or believed before. The good news here is that you ultimately don't have to accept the invitation.

The reflective questions for each invitation are designed for you try on each idea. Think of each invitation as an opportunity to see how it suits you. Does it fit? Does it feel uncomfortable, but something you would like to work on and grow into? Or, does the invitation feel completely wrong and not aligned for you?

If you thoughtfully answer each question, you will find that your insights will help you decide if the invitations are for you or not!

We invite you to also do this work with your team, as a coaching tool, or just for yourself. We have found that teams that do this work together, tremendously expand their connection and understanding for one another.

Have fun!

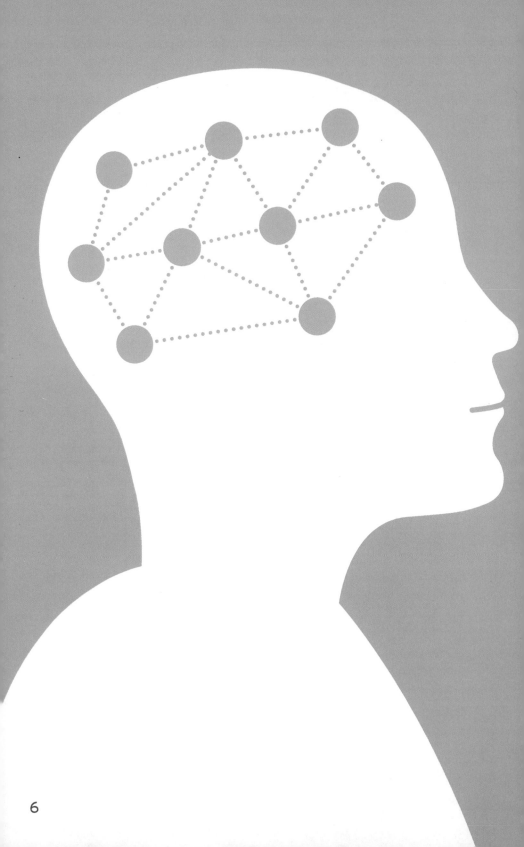

Invitation #1

Difficult people are not difficult until someone else believes that they are.

People cannot be difficult. People can demonstrate behavior that we may believe to be difficult to deal with, manage, work around, etc. But people themselves are not difficult. Complex, maybe—but not difficult.

Most of the 'difficult' people we encounter are just being who they are. They're busy being who they've always been. How they act. What they say. How they interact. Their behavior has been cultivated over a lifetime. Just like you and me, right? Each one of us behave in a manner that is learned from our experience. So, how they act isn't necessarily difficult. But because it is different from our expectation, we perceive it to be difficult.

As soon as we believe something or someone to be difficult, it impacts how we interact with them.

- What behaviors do I experiences as difficult?

- If you are currently experiencing a relationship you believe to be difficult, identify the key challenges in the relationship.

- What expectations do I have for how people should or shouldn't interact with me?

- Why do you think people should or shouldn't act in the ways you describe?

- What if other people's behavior had nothing to do with your own? How might that change how you interact with difficult people in your life or work?

- What are three other ways I can interpret _____'s behavior that don't contribute to the belief I have that they are difficult?

- Why do I choose to believe that someone is difficult?

- Why might I want to believe that someone is difficult?

- How do I believe _____ (insert difficult person's name, code name or nick name here) is impacting my work? My life?

- How do I believe _____'s behavior is impacting my ability to perform in my work?

9

Invitation #2

What we think about, comes about.

As Dennis Deaton says, "the eye sees what the mind looks for." As soon as we believe that someone is difficult, we seek out evidence to prove that we're correct. Most of the time, this isn't intentional. It's your brain needing to find correlation and support for your belief about the difficult person. And, because we spend most of our time thinking about how other people should or shouldn't behave with us, we spend very little time examining how we are reacting to them.

It takes two people to participate in a relationship. Rather than only entertaining how the difficult person should change, why not also entertain how you may be contributing to the relationship. In the book,"Change Your Think", we challenge managers to notice how their thinking impacts the results they get with their teams.

It flows like this
O

1. What I think drives how I feel.

2. How I feel drives how I act.

3. How I act leads to my results.

4. So, if I think that my colleague is difficult and hard to work with I may feel frustrated.

5. When I feel frustrated do I ignore, speak bluntly or curtly to him/her?

6. When I speak bluntly or curtly what kind of results might I get in the relationship?

7. When I ignore someone I work with, what kind of results might I get in the relationship?

Other people do not drive your behavior, your thoughts do.

To get a different result from yourself, you have to start thinking differently about this person and yourself in this relationship.

When you see them as an adversary, it's likely you will find them to be.

If you see them as a partner, it's likely you will find evidence to prove that true as well. You get to pick.

You may not like what other people do or say, but not liking how they behave is not an excuse for you to not accept accountability for how you behave. Stop waiting for them to change, in order for you to act differently. Your behavior is your choice, not a reaction to someone else. You alone are the one in charge of yourself and your results.
This is also true for the 'difficult' people. The only way they will ever change is if they choose to. Not because you want them to do so.

Reflections

- What are the primary thoughts I have about the difficult person I work with?

- Connect a feeling to each thought. For example: I think she is intentionally trying to hurt my career which makes me feel anger.

- Connect how you behave to each feeling. For example: When I feel anger my action or behavior is to be rude to her/him.

- What result do you get in the relationship when you do what you do? For example: When I am rude I don't connect or don't have constructive conversations.

- How might my behavior be contributing to the challenges in our relationship?

- What might I need to take accountability for in the relationship that I was previously blaming on the other person?

- How have I not been accepting responsibility for my own behavior?

- How would I prefer to act in the relationship?

- How might I need to feel to act this way?

- What do I need to believe about myself or the other person that makes me feel this way?

- What is one new thought I can choose to think that helps me take action that I feel good about?

Invitation #3

There will always be a difficult person. Always.

There are days you'd like to quit your job and mow the lawn at the local golf course. Anything to get away from (insert name here). But the truth is, there is always going to be **that** person. The more we resist dealing with them, the less likely we are to adapt and learn new skills for managing different personalities and perspectives.

We often explain the futility of resistance to our clients with this example: Let's take a walk to the beach in your mind. Let's say we stand, arm in arm, knee-deep in the waves. We tire of the waves. They thrash us around. They make it hard to stand in place. They are unpredictable and sometimes unexpectedly strong.

So, we decide we want the waves to stop rolling in. With a collective "STOP!", we yell at the waves to stop rolling in. We tell them that we're done with them and would like them to STOP right now! What happens? Well, unless it's the end of times, the waves continue to roll in.

This is what we do with people and circumstances in our lives. We focus on what we want to change, instead of working with "what is". The truth is, if you grow weary of the waves there are so many other options available to you, right?

- You can surf with a board

- You can body surf

- You can float

- You can dive through the waves

- You can go out past the break

- And you can even get out of the ocean all together. Always an option.

But making the ocean waves stop isn't one. And as long as we stand there yelling at the ocean to stop, we will not find solutions for working within the waves.

As long as you continue to yell in your mind about how someone should change or be different, you will not find a solution to work within the situation. You will only find more challenges. Just like waves, people are generally that consistent. Even if they are consistently inconsistent. We can usually plan on people being exactly like we've known them to be. Sometimes, we can almost chuckle when difficult people behave exactly as we expect them to. We may not choose them as a colleague, employee, or boss, but we can at least no longer pretend to be surprised when they act as they always do.

People don't change for your reasons; they change for their own. Yelling at them to be different doesn't work. Understanding this and accepting this invitation is probably one of the most liberating gifts you can give yourself.

Reflections

- What truth have I been resisting about this person or this relationship?

- What has been consistent that I wish would change?

- What am I resisting?

- What behavior do I think the other person needs to change in order for me to feel better?

- What might happen if I expected the other person to behave as they do, rather than spend my time wishing they would change?

- What can I change about the way I interact in this relationship?

- If the person is the ocean waves, what have I been "yelling" at them to change or stop doing? How likely is it that will happen?

- What can I change instead?

- What might happen if I choose to stop trying to change this person?

- Where else in my life do I rely on other people's behavior to determine how I feel?

- How do I feel when I interact with this person?

- How would I like to feel when I interact with this person?

Invitation #4

Everyone in your life is there for a 'season'.

If there's one thing we've learned, it is that people move on. Nothing is static. Making large professional and life decisions because of one person's behavior is something we encourage all of our clients to think long and hard about. People move on. It's very likely that the person that you want to escape is also making plans to do something new as well. And even if they aren't, nothing stays the same for long.

You have dreams, aspirations, and goals. Never let one person sway you from your ambitions. And, if you are finding that you are rattled by the behavior of someone else, it may be time to consider your goals.

Do you have a plan?

Do you know where you are going?

Do you know what you want to achieve in the next year, two years, three?

Clients who are the most unclear about their future are also the most impacted by difficult people in their lives.

When you don't have a plan for where you are going, it can make the challenges of today feel extremely big and unmanageable. But if you know the direction you are heading, it can help make the challenges of the day feel like blips on the radar and suddenly they are much more manageable.

Reflections

- For each area of your life make a list.

- Write down the topic on the top of the page. For example: Career.

- Underneath the topic write all of the things you don't want to have happen. Then for each thing you don't want, right a contrasting DO WANT. For example; I don't want to travel for my work. I do want to work from home.

- Doing this work can help you sort through those things that are most important.

- What are your top 5 life outcomes?

- For each outcome, go through the following questions.

- What will you need to accomplish in the next 20 years to accomplish this outcome?

- Next 10 years?

- Next 5 years?

- Next year?

- Next six months?

- Next 90 days?

- What do you really, really, really want in your career, life, love, health, etc.?

- What are you really, really, really willing to do to get it? Be specific.

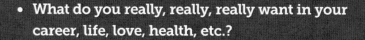

Invitation #5

You don't have to give up who you are to work with a difficult person.

But you may just have to learn new skills and challenge yourself to do more and be more for yourself and others. So often, clients believe that they have to over-compromise to get along with a difficult person. They believe they have to give up a part of who they are to make it work.

I see it quite differently: that you aren't giving anything up. You are a whole, complete person. What I've experienced instead is that when we encounter someone we believe to be difficult it is our cue to learn a new skill, manage ourselves and others differently and to embrace the discomfort and challenge to broaden our capabilities. Whether we need to do so in our conversations, our boundaries, our communication, or our technical skills.

5 Truths For Thinking About Difficult People   25

Reflections

- What new skills do you think you could learn to help you improve how you deal with difficult people?

- What skill are you overusing?

- What skill are you underusing that you have demonstrated in the past?

- Who do you know who is already good at these skills?

- What ideas do you have for learning and practicing the new skill(s)?

- How might your work change if you develop these skills?

- What is in it for you to do this work?

- Regardless of the current difficult relationship, what are five advantages to learning and practicing these new skills?

- If we are our own best advocate what might you tell yourself to encourage you to learn and practice these new skills?

- What have you learned or are you learning by knowing this difficult person?

Let's Rewind

You've just entertained five invitations. Five different ways to think about working with that "difficult" person.

- **Difficult people are not difficult until someone else believes that they are.**

- **What we think about, comes about.**

- **There will always be a difficult person. Always.**

- **Everyone in your life is there for a season.**

- **You don't have to give up who you are to work with a difficult person.**

It's up to you if you choose to accept any of them. Try them on for a while and see what you think. But whether or not you choose to change your perspective will not change the fact that there will always be another difficult person at work.

How you choose to react to these people and the relationships you create with them is ultimately up to you. Regardless of how they behave, your actions and your interactions are yours to keep.

Made in United States
Orlando, FL
06 January 2022

13071585R00018